DE
NV
ER

A
POEM
BY
KEN ARKIND

ILLUSTRATED
BY
CHARLY FASANO

DE NV ER

A
POEM
BY
KEN ARKIND

ILLUSTRATED
BY
CHARLY FASANO

On October 27, 2007 the Boston Red Sox defeated the Colorado Rockies 13-1 in Game 1 of the World Series. It was the highest scoring Game 1 in Major League Baseball history. It was the Rockies' first World Series appearance. The Red Sox swept the series 4-0.

That same year, Men's Health Magazine conducted a study to determine the drunkest cities in America. Denver took the top spot.

"Don't you ever call Denver the Midwest! Denver is the Wild West, motherfucker!"
- Jeanann Verlee

Denver, Colorado after Game 1 against the Red Sox

The D&F Clock Tower on 16th and Arapahoe used to be the tallest
    structure west of New York CIty.

A false idol to legitimacy
built by Old West mobsters trying to bring attention to what was considered
by most of the country
a train station piss pot before the West Coast.

Curtis was once called the "street of 10,000 lights,"
a six-block used condom of brothels, saloons and strip joints so brightly
lit you could always tell how much fun your neighbor had on Saturday
judging by their sunburn at Sunday services.

Colfax has always been Colfax,
an exposed artery in
dreams of western expansion,
sliced open by the Continental Divide,
when the blood pooled we called it home.

If New York is the city that never sleeps,
Denver is the city that passed out before last call.

Statistics say we drink twice as much as Boston
the proof is in the pavement,
if it wasn't for that pesky American Revolution
we'd have at least a bill's more bodies
scraped into the streets,
leaving behind the stink of all the wasted tax dollars
spent on drunk driving ads.

So have your World Series,
we never needed a reason to riot beyond our own elevation,
some people blame the altitude sickness,
but being that much closer to heaven
reminds you of how unreachable it actually is,
so we smear sins off on steering wheels
like wiping our feet on god's doormat.

Fuck your gravity.

Gravity is nothing but the bottom of god's boot.

It's nature's most polite form of violence.

We know gravity well,
live beneath the shadow of the back of its hand
with every hangover.

So do not call those mountains,
                    those are not mountains,
those are slow motion Gomorrah,
those are tidal waves of stone
                    and tonight the city is drowning.

In Lodo,
women dressed in their flyest meat hooks,
hold their mocha martini drooped profiles
in tonight's question marks,
searching for tomorrow's
answers in the form of men
who wear shirts that look like insurance companies.

Bar Bar pulsing like an epileptic heart rate
glasses breaking like gunshots
there's a dog on the pool table
the band's too drunk to play
and there's more smoke than a Teller County forest fire,
but when all the bartenders are under age, who gives a shit.

Across town in the Baker District,
black-scarfed hipsters talk about social network avatars,
as though they come from a big town,
and the band's not too drunk to play but the club's
too crowded to dance,
so the kids just set themselves on fire
and spread their ashes across the floor.

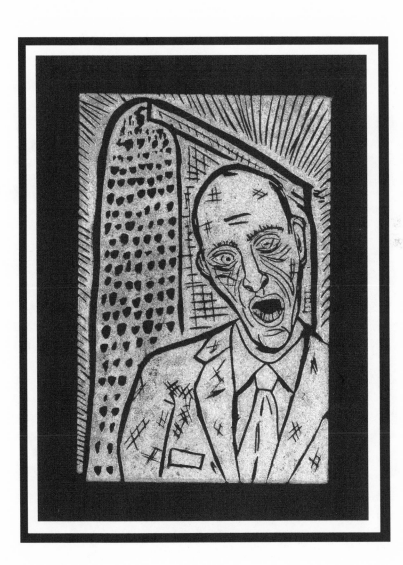

Colfax is still mopping up the blood,
and somewhere near the Bluebird Theater
a woman hollers:

"FUCK NO, I DON'T DRINK COORS!"

While I'm bouncing between bars
off 13th Avenue,
working on a tomorrow more hung-over
than a clothesline,
trying my best to forget the smell of somebody's hair
her golden curls,
sharp
and shining,
as the wire
with which heaven lines its gates.

Raising glasses in Denver is a middle finger against natural law.

It's a dream picking a fight with fact.

We still live in a cow town
but it's full of wolves
with hearts that pulse like neon signs,
and grins jagged the way eastbound streets
ricochet off of Five Points.

Our sunshine has been California's biggest cash crop since the gold
    rush
but we've always been better at screaming
thin air carries voices well
hangs in the wind like a savior.

We believe in fire more than prayer,
throwing Molotov cocktails at the sky,
till we can't tell the difference
between flames and stars.

We are tossing rocks at chain link fences
just to see a spark,
we are an unmarked cross
standing defiantly on the side of I-70,
we are a lit cigarette tossed from St. Christopher's
car window.

We are still bleeding.

We use Gun Club Road as a noose to the hang the memories
of our dead friends
scream their names
from our dust devil lungs
into the hollow stone heart
of Union Station,
then sharpen the pick axes of our teeth on the echo.

We are flames engulfing the hills of the West Side,
the last decade of gentrification ripping away,
a fur coat burning across an emaciated spine.

We are drinking whiskey until our throats are warm
and rough as the hands of Corky Gonzales.

We are the ghost of Don Becker's severed arm sobbing
like an abandoned lover,
and the cracked laughter of his final joke
stumbling through the alleyways of Capitol Hill
like a limping bullet.

We are human funeral piers
dancing in eulogy
watching the register building buckle
like an alcoholic's knees beneath the weight
of next years layoffs,
as the burning flags blowing atop the Brown Palace
clap in thunderous applause
and we run with flaming limbs
into the muddy waters of the Platte River,

baptizing ourselves again
and again,
until day breaks like last call.

The new light
shining upon windows, fractured
as a hobo island grin.

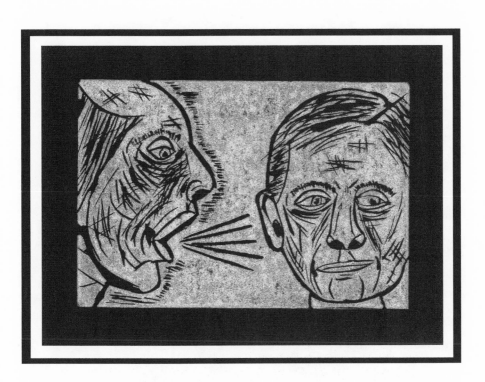

The streets
defeated as a Commerce City sunrise.

The shadows of the mountain tops receding into the west,
as though god's hand was folding,
his fingertips combing the eastern prairies like pack animals,

the morning skyline glinting like canines
the beasts howling as they go.

Ken Arkind is an American National Poetry Slam Champion, Tedx Fellow, Nuyorican Poets Cafe Grand Slam Champion and published poet who has performed his work in 49 States, 6 countries and at over 150 colleges and universities. He is the current Executive Director and head coach of Denver Minor Disturbance, an independent literary arts organization dedicated to helping Colorado youth find voice through the mediums of poetry and performance.

Charly "the city mouse" Fasano is a poet, block printer, and filmmaker from Ithaca, NY via Denver, Colorado. He is the founder of Fast Geek Press, Pretend You Can Reab audio zine, and As Well As Magazine. He has released a vinyl EP, a CD, two cassette tapes and four books of poems. Fasano's poems have appeared in Yellow Rake Zine, Lubricated Magazine, Growing Strange Magazine and This Ain't No Cowtown Compilation: Number Two. His films and music videos have appeared at prickofthespindle.com, movingpoems.com, Westword.com and The Onion's AV Club online.

Made in the USA
Charleston, SC
28 March 2013